Let's Walk to School

Written by DEBORAH CHANCELLOR

Illustrated by DIANE EWEN

CRABTREE
PUBLISHING COMPANY
WWW.CRABTREEBOOKS.COM

Before, During, and After Reading Prompts

Activate Prior Knowledge and Make Predictions

Read the title of the book to the children and look at the illustrations. Ask children what they think the book may be about. Ask them questions related to the title, such as:

- How do you get to school? What about soccer practice, music class, or grandma's house?
- Do you take walks with your family? When?

During Reading

Stop at various points during reading and ask children questions related to the story:

- Why doesn't Tom want to walk to school? *(see pages 4, 14, 16)*
- Why is the drive to school so slow? *(see pages 10–11, 18–19)*
- Why does the air smell so bad? *(see pages 10–11)*
- Why is walking good for the environment? *(see pages 14–15)*

- Why does Mom decide to stop driving Tom to school? *(see pages 18–19)*
- What happens when Tom walks to school? *(see pages 24–25)*

After Reading

Look at the information panels, then talk together about air pollution. Ask children the following prompting questions:

- How can walking help cut down on air pollution? *(see page 9)*
- What causes air pollution? *(see page 11)*
- What does air pollution lead to? *(see page 15)*
- What are some effects of global warming? *(see page 17)*
- How can you help to reduce air pollution and the amount of traffic on the roads? *(see page 21)*

Do the Quiz together *(see pages 28–29)*. Refer back to the information panels to find answers.

Crabtree Publishing Company

www.crabtreebooks.com   1-800-387-7650

Published in Canada
Crabtree Publishing
616 Welland Ave.
St. Catharines, Ontario
L2M 5V6

Published in the United States
Crabtree Publishing
PMB 59051
350 Fifth Avenue, 59th Floor
New York, New York 10118

First published in 2019 by Wayland (an imprint of Hachette Children's Group, part of Hodder and Stoughton)
Copyright © Hodder and Stoughton, 2019

Author: Deborah Chancellor
Illustrator: Diane Ewen
Editorial Director: Kathy Middleton
Editors: Sarah Peutrill, Ellen Rodger
Designer: Cathryn Gilbert
Print and production coordinator: Katherine Berti

Printed in the U.S.A./122019/CG20191101

Library and Archives Canada Cataloguing in Publication

Title: Let's walk to school / written by Deborah Chancellor ; illustrated by Diane Ewen.
Other titles: Let us walk to school
Names: Chancellor, Deborah, author. | Ewen, Diane (Illustrator), illustrator.
Description: Series statement: Good to be green |
  Previously published: London: Wayland, 2019. |
  Includes index. | "A story about why it's important to walk more".
Identifiers: Canadiana (print) 20190194324 |
  Canadiana (ebook) 20190194332 |
  ISBN 9780778772835 (hardcover) | ISBN 9780778772903 (softcover) |
  ISBN 9781427124715 (HTML)
Subjects: LCSH: Motor vehicles—Motors—Exhaust gas—Environmental
  aspects—Juvenile literature. | LCSH: Air—Pollution—Juvenile literature. |
  LCSH: Walking—Juvenile literature. | LCSH: Sustainable living—Juvenile
  literature. | LCSH: Environmentalism—Juvenile literature.
Classification: LCC TD886.5 .C53 2020 | DDC j363.739/2—dc23

Library of Congress Cataloging-in-Publication Data

CIP available at the Library of Congress
LCCN: 2019043909

Let's Walk to School

A story about why it's important to walk more.

"Time to go!"
said Mom.

Tom was hiding.
"I don't like school,"
he said. "I want to
stay at home."

"I can't leave you here," said Mom. "I have to go to work."

Tom made a face.
"I'll drive you there,"
said Mom.

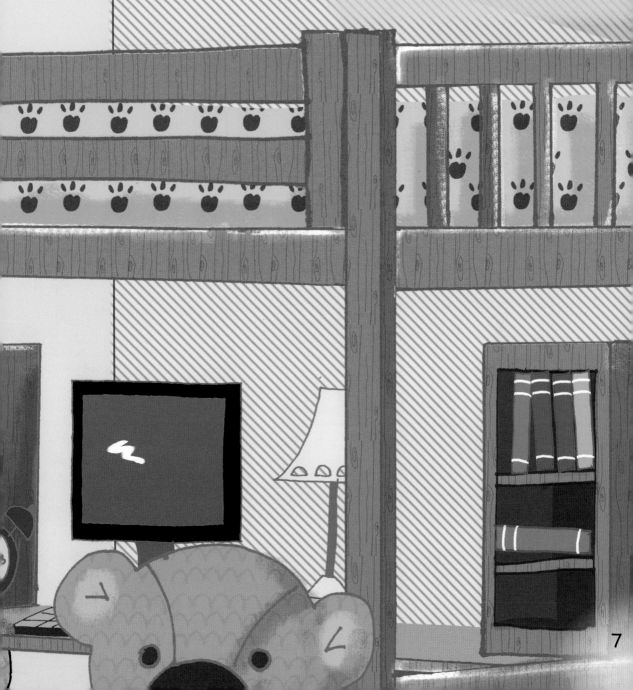

Tom got dressed in a hurry.
He got in the car and Mom
started the engine.

On short trips we can walk, ride a bike, skateboard, or scooter to save **fuel** and reduce **pollution**. This is good for the **environment**.

Soon they were stuck in a traffic jam.

Tom closed the car window.

"The air smells terrible!" he said.

"That's because of the exhaust fumes," said Mom.

Exhaust fumes from vehicles pollute the air we breathe. Factories and **power stations** do too. Also, they all release **greenhouse gases** that trap heat near Earth. Even cows on dairy farms burp and fart a greenhouse gas!

"It's so hot!" said Tom.
"Our summers are getting
hotter," said Mom.

"Air pollution is heating up Earth.
This is called **global warming**."
Tom didn't like the sound of this.

"Let's walk to school tomorrow," said Mom.
"Walking is good for the environment
because it doesn't make any pollution."
"But it's too hot to walk!" said Tom.

Pollution and greenhouse gases rise into Earth's **atmosphere**, trapping some of the Sun's rays. This warms up Earth's surface and changes weather patterns.

So the next day, Mom drove Tom
to school again. There was a
big thunderstorm. "Let's walk to
school tomorrow," said Mom.
"But it's too wet to walk!" said Tom.

Global warming is slowly changing our **climate**, causing more extreme weather around the world, such as **droughts**, storms, and **floods**.

So the next day, Mom drove Tom to school again. They got stuck in the worst traffic jam, ever.

"I've had enough of this!" said Mom.
"No excuses—you're walking to
school tomorrow!"

"I'm going to take the train to work," said Mom. "And you can walk, whatever the weather is like."

You can help reduce traffic on the roads by walking or taking **public transportation**, such as trains, buses, street cars, and subways.

The next day, Mom left the car at home. She took the train to work, and Tom set off for school on foot.

Walking and cycling keeps us fit and healthy. It makes our muscles strong and is good for our hearts. It keeps our brains active, too!

At first, Tom wasn't very happy. But then he met a girl called Fen on the way. The walk was fun.

24

"Let's walk to school tomorrow," said Fen.
Tom liked the sound of this.

Mom got home from work early.
"My train was so quick!" she said.
"How was school?"

"It was fun," said Tom.
"And from now on, I'm going
to walk to school every day!"

Quiz time

Which of these things
are true? Read the book
again to find out!

*(Cover up the answers
on page 29.)*

1. Air pollution is only caused by traffic jams.

2. Air pollution is bad for the environment.

3. Our climate is changing because of global warming.

4. Public transportation adds to all the traffic on the roads.

5. Walking is bad for you, because it makes you tired.

Answers

1. **False**
Traffic fumes are not the only cause of air pollution. Factories, power stations and cattle burps add to the problem. *(See page 11)*

2. **True**
Air pollution and greenhouse gases rise into the atmosphere, trapping the Sun's rays. This warms Earth's surface, changing weather patterns. *(See page 15)*

3. **True**
Global warming is heating up Earth. This is changing our climate and bringing more extreme weather, such as floods and droughts. *(See page 17)*

4. **False**
If more people took trains and buses, there would be fewer cars on the roads, and less traffic. *(See page 21)*

5. **False**
Walking and cycling keeps you fit and healthy. It is good for the environment, too. *(See page 23)*

Get active

In the story, Tom and his mom change the way they do things to help the environment—Tom starts walking to school and Mom takes the train to work. Do you make any unnecessary car journeys? Can you think of another way to make those journeys?

Ask an adult to take you on a bus or train ride. Take some photos and put together a photo story of your trip when you get home. You could add speech bubbles to make your story more fun to read!

Ask your friends: Who walks to school? Who goes by bus? Who goes by train? Who gets a ride in a car? Make a bar chart to show how many people do each activity. What is the most common way people get to school?

Air pollution adds to the problems of global warming and climate change. Look out for stories in the news about extreme weather around the world, for example hurricanes, floods, and droughts. Make a collage of dangerous weather events that may be made worse by global warming.

A note about sharing this book

The *Good to Be Green* series provides a starting point for further discussion on important environmental issues, such as pollution, climate change, and endangered wildlife. Each topic is relevant to both children and adults.

Let's Walk to School

This story explores some issues surrounding air pollution. *Let's Walk to School* includes practical suggestions for how to reduce air pollution, such as choosing to walk rather than travel by car, or choosing to travel long distances by train. The information panels in the book cover the wider issue of global warming, explaining in simple terms its causes and global effects.

The story and nonfiction elements in *Let's Walk to School* encourage the reader to conclude that we should all walk or cycle, whenever possible, or use public transportation. This helps to reduce air pollution and also saves fuel.

How to use the book

Adults can share this book with individuals or groups of children, and use it as a starting point for discussion. Illustrations provide visual support for children who are starting to read on their own. This book also uses repetition to reinforce understanding. For example, the phrase "let's walk to school tomorrow" is repeated throughout the book. The positive ending of the story is emphasized when the earlier sentence, "Tom didn't like the sound of this," is changed to "Tom liked the sound of this."

The story introduces vocabulary relevant to the theme of air pollution, such as: *atmosphere, climate, drought, engine, environment, factories, fuel, fumes, global warming, greenhouse gases, pollution, power station, public transportation*. Unfamiliar vocabulary is in bold text, and defined in the glossary on page 32. When reading the story for the first time, refer to the glossary with the children.

There is also an index on page 32. Encourage children to use the index when you are talking about the book. For example, ask them to use the index to find the pages that describe global warming (pages 13, 15, 17). It is important that children know that information can be found in books as well as searched for on the Internet with a responsible adult.

Glossary

atmosphere The air around Earth

climate Pattern of weather over a long period of time

droughts Long periods of time without rain

environment The world around us

exhaust fumes Pollution that comes from burning fuel, such as gas, in vehicles

floods Large amounts of water overflowing into areas that are normally dry

fuel Material (such as gas or oil) burned for heat or power

global warming The rising temperature of Earth's surface, caused by air pollution

greenhouse gases Gases such as carbon dioxide and methane that trap the Sun's heat near Earth

pollution Harmful chemicals that make a place or thing dirty

power station The place where electric power is created and sent out

public transportation Ways of getting around that many people can use at the same time, such as buses and trains

Index